Flowers of the Norfolk Coast

Simon Harrap

Norfolk Nature *Guides*

CONTENTS

ACKNOWLEDGEMENTS

I would like to thank Anne Harrap, Tony Leech. Nigel Redman and Lenny Thompson for reading through the text and making many useful comments and corrections, Bob Ellis for answering my queries regarding Norfolk plants, and Richard Porter for sharing his data on Blakeney Point.

Published in 2008 by Norfolk Nature,
1 Holt Road, Edgefield, Melton Constable, Norfolk NR24 2RP

www.norfolknature.co.uk

ISBN 978-0-9558579-0-4

Designed by Simon Harrap
Printed by Barnwell Print Ltd, Aylsham, Norfolk

Introduction

Norfolk is a fantastic county for wildlife, perhaps the best. Contributing greatly to its attraction for wildlife is its extraordinarily long and varied coastline, much of which is protected by a string of national and international designations. Along the entire length of this coast there are wild flowers to be seen, from the glorious blaze of colour produced by the massed sea-lavenders to the subtle beauty of little clovers or the sombre hues of a December reed bed. It is a great place to look at, study and enjoy wild flowers.

From the many hundreds of species of flower that can be found along the Norfolk coast I have selected 77 to describe and illustrate. These include most of the seaside specialists, the plants that make their home nowhere else, as well as some more widespread flowers that are especially conspicuous on the coast. Most should be easy to find and to recognise, but some are subtler or more elusive; others have been included to attract the readers' attention and stimulate their interest.

I hope that this book will open the eyes of both Norfolk residents and visitors to the wonderful flowers that can be found here. Plants are essential to human life, providing the food that we eat and the oxygen that we breathe. Despite this, they are neglected, even by wildlife enthusiasts. The Royal Society for the Protection of Birds (RSPB) has over a million members, Plantlife, the wild plant conservation charity, just 12,000. This book aims to help redress this imbalance.

Seaside Plants

On the coast the flora is dominated by the wind and the sea. The wind, as well as affecting the form and shape of many plants, has a drying effect that many 'softer' species cannot survive. The sea also promotes desiccation as its salts encourage the flow of water out of the plant through osmosis. Wind and sea combine to make the coast a harsh environment and coastal specialists have a range of adaptations to protect themselves. Some are low-growing, hugging the ground to keep out of the wind. Many have a thick, waxy cuticle on the leaves or a covering of fine hairs, both of which help to reduce water loss. Some have reduced the size of the leaves to cut down on the area vulnerable to dessication. Often seaside plants are fleshier and more succulent than their relatives inland, the leaves and stem having a greater capacity to store water. All of these adaptations to survive a harsh, drying environment are shared with plants that grow in the arid regions of the world and it is not surprising that some of Norfolk's coastal flowers also grow in semi-desert regions or have close relatives there. Some, such as Thrift and Sea Campion, are also found in another harsh, windy environment – high mountains. The sea does, however, have positive effects. It moderates the temperature and keeps the winters mild. Even in these days of global warming, plants on the coast will come into flower somewhat earlier than those even just a mile or two inland.

Coastal Habitats

The vegetation in Britain has been heavily influenced by man for thousands of years and there are very few places where the vegetation is not the direct result of human activity. Even 'wild' habitats, such as woods and fens, heaths and moors, would not be in their present form without human interference. Coastal habitats are, however, more-or-less natural. Norfolk's beaches and dunes, the great shingle ridge on the north coast, and the vast swathes of saltmarsh on the Wash, the north coast and around Breydon Water are all natural. Coastal defence works, the drainage of some areas and a lack of large grazing animals have all affected them in some way but, in essence, they look pretty much the same as they would have done thousands of years ago. Although not pristine, they are as natural as a tropical rainforest or an Arctic wilderness.

Beaches

Norfolk beaches are the front line against the sea. Perhaps the most inhospitable of coastal habitats for plants, nothing can survive for long below the high water mark, especially during a winter storm. Yet, along and just above the strandline – that fascinating line of debris, both natural and man-made, that marks the furthest extent of the tides – there will be a line of vegetation. Annuals such as Saltwort, Sea Rocket and Frosted Orache take advantage of summer's kinder weather to grow and set seed, while the decay of the debris left by the tides provides a source of nutrients.

Dunes

At the top of the beach, above the strandline, may be scattered tufts of a tough perennial grass Sand Couch, and these are the key to dune formation. Dunes are formed by wind-blown sand but, for a dune to start forming, there has to be something to stop the sand. Sand Couch is the first really permanent obstacle to the sand's passage and as sand builds up around the grass it starts to build a low fore-dune. It is another grass, however, Marram, that does the real job of dune-building. Marram can grow up through the accumulating sand and as it grows its mass of tough roots and rhizomes binds the sand together. In this way dunes can reach a considerable height – the tallest in Norfolk are on Blakeney Point, Scolt Head Island and at Gun Hill.

Dunes show a transition of vegetation types. On the more mobile seaward side, exposed to the wind, the 'yellow dunes' are dominated by Marram and Sea Couch, together with Sea-holly, Sea Sandwort or Sea Bindweed. Moving inland, they become progressively stabler and the surface of these 'grey dunes' may be covered with fine turf or close-packed lichens. In these conditions trees and shrubs can grow and there are sometimes thickets of Sea-buckthorn or, as at Holkham, the dunes have been planted with pines. Dune grassland holds many interesting plants, such as Common Centaury and Hound's-tongue, but the range of species present is determined in part by the soil chemistry. Some dunes are more alkaline, favouring Pyramidal and Bee Orchids, whilst others are more acid and may support heathland plants such as heather and gorse.

Dune Slacks

The hollows between the high dunes may be near the water-table and these dune slacks are wet, at least in winter, supporting plants that like marshy conditions. Again, the range of plants depends upon the chemistry of the water and some of the most interesting dune slacks are found where there are alkaline conditions; the slacks at Wells and Holkham hold concentrations of orchids and the massed ranks of Marsh Helleborines and Southern Marsh Orchids are one of Norfolk's wildlife spectacles.

The Shingle Bank

Extending from Weybourne towards the tip of Blakeney Point is a bank of shingle. The loose stones are a difficult place for plants to gain a foothold, but the shingle holds some great flowers, including Sea Campion and Biting Stonecrop, but the most iconic is Yellow Horned-poppy. In recent years the shingle bank has been greatly disturbed in an attempt to maintain it against the sea, with huge bulldozers working to push the shingle into a high ridge. This has destroyed many plants, but has now been abandoned as futile and the bank will be naturally re-profiled by

the sea. To the rear of the bank there is an area of saline mud and pools, heavily influenced by salt water coming over the top of the shingle or seeping through it, and this holds an excellent selection of saltmarsh plants.

Saltmarshes

North Norfolk has been dubbed the 'saltmarsh coast' and holds some fantastic unspoilt saltmarshes. A saltmarsh forms where the sea holds a load of fine sediment and the coast is sufficiently sheltered, by spits and sandbars, for the water to be calm enough for silt to settle to the bottom. One further ingredient is required, however, and that is plants, which trap this sediment and prevent it being washed away on the next tide; in this way the surface of the saltmarsh builds up. It is a very slow process, however, with a fine balance between the amount of silt deposited around the saltmarsh plants and the quantity of material washed away by the sea. Some of Norfolk's saltmarshes are 6,000 years old.

Dominated by the tides, saltmarshes provide a range of opportunities for plants. The difference between high and low water may be over 5 m on a spring tide, but as little as 1.8 m on a neap tide. Spring and neap tides have a fortnightly cycle as the moon waxes and wanes and superimposed on this rhythm are annual variations, with particularly big tides around the spring and autumn equinoxes.

The result of these variations in the height of the tide is that parts of the saltmarsh are inundated by seawater every day, and others only a couple of times a fortnight, while the very highest parts may be covered just a few times a year. Clearly, this provides a range of conditions, with glassworts (samphire) the pioneers, colonising fresh mud on the lowest, wettest parts of the marsh, and Sea-purslane and Sea Wormwood on the higher and drier zones. The saltmarsh also has structure. The sides of the drainage channels provide different conditions to the open marsh, and there are also pans. These are bare, often circular ponds and as these dry out over the space of the fortnight between the higher tides the concentration of salt becomes extremely high, making them very inhospitable to plants. Often only the highly specialised samphire can survive these conditions.

Cliffs

Norfolk lacks dramatic high cliffs, but does nevertheless have some very interesting cliff habitats. In the west, the cliffs at Hunstanton are relatively hard and hold few plants, although the grassland on the clifftop can be interesting. In the east cliffs extend from Sheringham to Mundesley and are much softer. Their tumbled slopes hold specialities such as Thrift and Sea-buckthorn, while some sections are ablaze with Kidney Vetch in the summer. It is the slumped, clay cliffs between Cromer and Mundesley, however, which hold the greatest interest, for here there are numerous seepages of fresh chalky water and these support many orchids, notably the reddish form of Early Marsh Orchid (a British endemic).

Conservation

None of the plants featured in this book are specially protected, and in general for the commoner species it is perfectly acceptable to pick a flower or leaf for a closer look – indeed, this is one of the best ways to learn your flowers. Brief notes are included on the culinary uses of some plants, and a few handfuls of samphire or a bunch of Alexanders is unlikely to harm the populations of these abundant species. The scarcer species should be left alone, however, and it should be noted that it is illegal to uproot any plant without the land owner's permission (and thus collecting samphire by uprooting the whole plant is, strictly speaking, illegal).

You can help to conserve wild flowers in two ways. Firstly by supporting the work of the Norfolk Wildlife Trust (www.norfolkwildlifetrust.org.uk) and Plantlife (www.plantlife.org.uk). Secondly, by helping with the recording and monitoring of wild plants and thus helping to provide the essential data upon which all conservation should be based. The Norfolk and Norwich Naturalists' Society is the organisation for every keen naturalist in Norfolk, and details of the Norfolk plant recorders can be found on their website: www.nnns.org.uk.

YELLOW HORNED-POPPY *Glaucium flavum*

One of the signature plants of the Norfolk coast, especially the huge sweep of shingle between Weybourne and Blakeney Point.

IDENTIFICATION Distinctive at all times. In winter the tough rosettes of deeply lobed, crimped, grey-green leaves are just about the only plants to show any signs of life on the shingle bank, while in summer the bright yellow flowers and extraordinarily long, sickle-shaped seed pods (the 'horns') demand attention. **HABITAT** Shingle banks and beaches. **DISTRIBUTION** Common on the Wash coast between Wolferton and Heacham and on the N coast on Scolt Head Island and from Blakeney Point to Weybourne. Old records from Holme (1964) and Wells to Brancaster (*c.* 1796) indicate that suitable shingle habitat was once more extensive. Away from Norfolk widespread on British coasts, although absent from most of Scotland and N and W Ireland.

Key features
- Stems to 90 cm long, but multi-branched and spreading; hairless
- Leaves lobed, the lower leaves deeply so, grey-green, slightly fleshy, downy
- Flowers 6-9 cm across

Key facts
- Biennial to perennial
- Flowers Jun-Sep
- When broken, exudes a yellow latex
- Poisonous
- Seed capsule 15-30 cm long, pencil-thin, distinctly curved

ORACHES are rather drab, weedy-looking annuals that love areas rich in nutrients; on the coast they favour the band of rotting debris left by the tide along the strandline, while inland they are often found around manure heaps. Their tiny flowers appear Jul-Oct and are either male, with 5 green sepals and 5 stamens (but no petals), or female, lacking both petals and sepals but enclosed by bracteoles, more or less triangular flaps that enlarge and swell as the seed ripens, and often become rather spongy (see right). In the rather similar goosefoots *Chenopodium*, a genus that includes the familiar weed Fat-hen *C. album*, each flower has both male and female structures and lacks bracteoles.

SPEAR-LEAVED ORACHE
Atriplex prostrata

The commonest orache on the coast, this species is very variable and can be upright and robust or dainty and sprawling (as below); the whole plant often turns red in the autumn. **IDENTIFICATION** Lower leaves always triangular, with the base making a right-angle with its stalk. Upright plants can reach 1 m, but prostrate plants are much smaller. Often looks rather 'mealy', as if it has excreted tiny grains of salt. **HABITAT** The strandline on beaches, saltmarsh margins and along sea walls, as well as damp saline flats behind the shingle bank. **DISTRIBUTION** Common along much of Norfolk's coast and widespread inland around manure heaps and, increasingly, along salted roads. Common throughout Britain.

GRASS-LEAVED ORACHE *Atriplex littoralis*

More of a seaside specialist than Spear-leaved Orache, but almost as common along the coast. **IDENTIFICATION** Leaves all narrow and strap-shaped. Although sometimes toothed, they never have triangular basal lobes. Growth erect, to 50-100 cm tall. **HABITAT** The strandline on beaches and along the edge of saltmarshes and sea walls. **DISTRIBUTION** Common along Norfolk's coast and widespread around all British coasts, also increasingly found inland along salted roads, especially in East Anglia.

FROSTED ORACHE
Atriplex laciniata

This attractive, 'sugar-frosted' orache is a characteristic plant of the strandline, typically growing together with Saltwort, Sea Sandwort and Sea Rocket. Described as 'rare' in the 1968 *Flora of Norfolk*, it has increased and spread markedly in recent years. **IDENTIFICATION** The silver-white frosted foliage and contrasting reddish stems are distinctive. Grows up to 30 cm tall, but rather spreading. Leaves diamond-shaped with wavy edges. **HABITAT** Sandy beaches. **DISTRIBUTION** Found along the entire Norfolk coast, although more scattered in the E, and similarly widespread around all British coasts.

SEA-PURSLANE *Atriplex portulacoides*

One of the most characteristic plants of the saltmarsh, this small shrub, which is closely-related to the oraches, has distinctive pale, grey-green foliage.

IDENTIFICATION Easily identified by the combination of its pale colour and spoon-shaped leaves; Sea Wormwood is more silvery and has finely cut leaves (see p. 52). **HABITAT** Saltmarshes, where typically forms dense stands in discrete zones along the fringes of pools and creeks. **DISTRIBUTION** Widespread and often abundant around the Wash, on the N coast as far east as Weybourne, and on the tidal rivers around Breydon Water, plus a few sites in NE Norfolk. Elsewhere in Britain common on the coasts of England, Wales, SW Scotland and Ireland, and slowly spreading northwards.

Key features
- Stems woody, to 1 m long, and well-branched
- Lower leaves elliptical, upper leaves narrower
- Flowers tiny, mostly either male or female
- Male flowers have 5 sepals and conspicuous yellow stamens, female flowers have no petals or sepals but 2 enveloping bracteoles that enlarge as the fruit develops

Key facts
- Perennial, evergreen
- The fleshy leaves can be used in salads or cooked like Spinach, and were once pickled
- Flowers Jul-Sep

SEA BEET *Beta vulgaris*

Usually looking somewhat scruffy, this unprepossessing plant is of great economic importance. The wild plant is edible, but its claim to fame is as the wild ancestor of Sugar Beet, Beetroot, Mangel-wurzel, Spinach and Swiss Chard, and the species was probably taken into cultivation in the Middle East over 2,000 years ago.

IDENTIFICATION The large, glossy, leathery leaves and red-striped stems are distinctive. **HABITAT** The upper margins of saltmarshes and the fringes of tidal rivers and sea walls; particularly enjoys the nutrient-rich debris marking the limit of the highest tides (or the passage of dogs). **DISTRIBUTION** Common around the Wash, on the N coast as far east as Salthouse and around Breydon Water, but absent from NE Norfolk and scarce on the E coast. Elsewhere in Britain widespread on the coast north to Yorkshire and SW Scotland.

Key features
- Grows to 1 m, but longer stems often collapsing
- Whole plant hairless,
- Stems often tinged red
- Leaves shiny and rather fleshy, the lower diamond-shaped to oblong, the upper leaves smaller and narrower

Key facts
- Perennial
- Flowers tiny, bisexual, with 2 stigmas and 5 green to reddish sepals.
- Wind-pollinated
- Edible, the leaves can be cooked as Spinach
- Flowers Jun-Sep

GLASSWORTS *Salicornia sp.* (aka 'SAMPHIRE')

The signature plant of the Norfolk coast, the massed ranks of short green shoots, often turning red, orange or yellow in autumn, lend a splash of late colour to the saltmarsh. Highly specialised, glassworts appear to lack leaves and to be merely jointed, succulent stems, but leaves are present in the form of pairs of triangular scale-like lobes tightly clasping opposite sides of the stem. Glassworts can be divided into two groups: seven annual species in the genus *Salicornia*, and the much more local Perennial Glasswort, genus *Sarcocornia*. Glasswort is the 'correct' English name and derives from their former use in glass-making (the ash is high in silica), but 'Samphire' (or 'Marsh Samphire') is much more commonly used in Norfolk (the word derives from '*Saint Pierre*', who walked on water). There has been a revival in the culinary uses of Samphire which

Key features
- Stems grow to 45 cm, often much branched
- Stems constricted or even 'beaded'
- Flowers tiny, comprising a fleshy disc, emerging from behind the 'leaves' with the tiny anther extruded from a central pore (the stigma remains hidden)
- Most species have flowers in groups of 3, with the central one the largest, but One-flowered Glasswort *S. pusilla* has a single flower
- **Key facts**
- Annual
- Edible, young shoots can be pinched off above the root and eaten raw. Later in the year the whole plant can be cooked and eaten like asparagus
- Flowers Aug-Sep

has led to its reappearance for sale at the side of the road and on TV cookery programmes. **IDENTIFICATION** The segmented stems, often well-branched but apparently lacking leaves, make identification as a glasswort straightforward; Annual Sea-blite is similar but has the leaves and stem clearly distinct (see p. 15). Glassworts are frustrating for keen botanists, however, because the different species of *Salicornia* (and there are seven in Norfolk), together with their numerous hybrids, are *very* hard to distinguish without prolonged study. For most purposes they are therefore best left as *Salicornia* sp. **HABITAT** The saltmarsh pioneers, glassworts colonise bare mud on the lower saltmarsh, on creek margins and in salt pans, as well as bare brackish ground behind the shingle bank. **DISTRIBUTION**

Found around the Wash, on the N coast east to Kelling, and along the tidal rivers around Breydon Water, and locally abundant. Similarly widespread away from Norfolk.

PERENNIAL GLASSWORT *Sarcocornia perennis*

Known locally as 'Sheep's Samphire', this species is not gathered for the table. **IDENTIFICATION** Can be identified with care by the presence of both flowering and non-flowering shoots that arise from a creeping rootstock to form large tussocks. **HABITAT** Found locally on firm, raised areas on the saltmarsh edge, where sand or gravel are mixed with the mud. **DISTRIBUTION** Confined to the N coast between Holme and Blakeney Point, where it is uncommon. Outside Norfolk also scarce, and restricted to the region SE of a line from the Wash to Devon, with outposts in W Wales and SE Ireland.

Key features
- Stems grow to 30 cm, but often sprawling
- As in many of the Salicornias, mature plants turn yellowish to reddish
- Flowers in groups of 3, about equal in size

Key facts
- Perennial
- Not palatable
- Flowers Aug-Sep

SHRUBBY SEA-BLITE *Suaeda vera*

Often known simply as 'suaeda', this salt-tolerant shrub forms dense thickets along parts of the Norfolk coast (e.g. Blakeney Point). In Europe it is largely Mediterranean in distribution, and its world range extends south to Angola and east to semi-desert areas in Central Asia and India; indeed, it reaches its northernmost limit in Britain.

IDENTIFICATION The shrubby habit, dense evergreen foliage and short, succulent leaves are distinctive. Young plants can resemble Annual Sea-blite, but have leaves that are rounded in cross-section and usually also rather shorter. **HABITAT** Grows along and above the high-water strandline on shingle banks and beaches and alongside sea walls, and also on raised ground in and around saltmarshes. **DISTRIBUTION** Confined to the Wash and the N coast as far east as Sheringham, and locally abundant. Elsewhere in Britain, as a native, the species is confined to Lincolnshire, Suffolk, Essex and Dorset, and is scarce.

Key features
- Evergreen, perennial
- Grows to 1.2 m high
- Leaves cylindrical in cross-section, 5-18 mm long, rounded at base and tip
- Flowers tiny, 1-2 mm across, with 5 succulent green sepals, 5 stamens and 3 stigmas

Key facts
- Seeds dispersed by the sea, germinating in the spring
- Stems buried deeply under shingle by winter storms 'layer' and produce new shoots
- Flowers Jul-Sep

ANNUAL SEA-BLITE *Suaeda maritima*

A very variable plant that is superficially similar to the glassworts and which may similarly turn a gorgeous shade of red in the autumn, but unlike glassworts its leaves are clearly distinct from the wiry stems.

IDENTIFICATION Smaller than Shrubby Sea-blite, with leaves that are distinctly semicircular in cross-section. **HABITAT** Saltmarshes, where often a pioneer species, growing on relatively bare mud together with a variety of glassworts. Also found on muddy shingle and other bare, wet, brackish ground (e.g. behind the shingle bank at Salthouse). **DISTRIBUTION** Widespread around the coasts of Britain and Ireland and in Norfolk occurs around the Wash and along the N coast as far east as Weybourne, and also along the tidal rivers around Breydon Water.

Key features
- Annual, but stem often rather woody at base
- Grows to 30 cm (rarely more), but often prostrate
- Leaves semicircular in cross-section, 3-25 mm long, pointed at tip
- Flowers tiny, as Shrubby Sea-blite but usually with just 2 stigmas

Key facts
- Can be eaten in salads, but rather salty
- Flowers Jul-Sep

PRICKLY SALTWORT *Salsola kali*

A very distinctive plant of the strandline, greyish-green with tiny, inconspicuous flowers, but definitely prickly to touch.

IDENTIFICATION The spine-tipped leaves are distinctive. **HABITAT** Grows along the strandline at the top of sandy beaches. **DISTRIBUTION** Found in Norfolk wherever there are suitable sandy beaches, but sparsely distributed on the E coast and absent from the shingle and cliffs between Blakeney Point and Cromer. Elsewhere occurs around all British coasts, but rare in N Scotland and has declined sharply in the S where beaches are used intensively for recreation.

Key features
- Stems branched, 20-40 cm long, usually somewhat prostrate, bristly, often striped with red
- Leaves succulent, bristly, short and strap-shaped, tapering to a spine at the tip
- Flowers tiny, enclosed by a pair of bracts, with 5 sepals

Key facts
- Annual
- Coastal plants belong to subspecies *kali*
- Inland, the subspecies *ruthenica*, a spineless form, is a rare alien 'tumbleweed' found on fields and waste ground
- Flowers Jul-Oct

SEA SANDWORT *Honckenya peploides*

One of the pioneers of the open shore, numerous shoots grow up each spring from a network of creeping rhizomes to form low-growing patches, and these are sometimes extensive, covering several square metres.

IDENTIFICATION The small whitish flowers are not eye-catching, but the small yellowish-green leaves, fleshy but stiff and geometrically arranged into tiers, are distinctive, as are the conspicuous pea-like fruits. **HABITAT** Areas of bare sand or sandy shingle above the high-water mark on beaches and dunes. **DISTRIBUTION** Common, it is only absent from the Wash coast south from Snettisham and from the cliffs between Weybourne and East Runton. Away from Norfolk distributed around all British coasts.

Key features
- Stems to 25 cm, but usually low-growing
- Flowers 6-10 mm across, with 5 sepals and 5 greenish-white petals
- Fruit a globular yellowish-green capsule
- Leaves oval with a pointed tip

Key facts
- Perennial, deciduous.
- Flowers hermaphrodite or, more often, with male and female flowers on different plants (i.e. dioecious)
- Male flowers have 10 stamens and petals about as long as sepals
- Female flowers have 3 styles and petals much shorter than sepals
- In parts of N England the leaves were once pickled and eaten
- Flowers May-Aug

GREATER SEA-SPURREY *Spergularia media*

Sea-spurreys are members of the pink family. Their pallid little star-shaped flowers wink up at you from amongst the drab greys, greens and browns of the saltmarsh, where their delicate blooms are regularly covered by the tide, apparently with no ill-effects. Two species occur in Norfolk and are often found growing together.

IDENTIFICATION Distinguished by the size of the flowers, and even more so by the relative length of the petals and sepals; in Greater the petals are longer than the sepals. Also tends to have whiter, more washed-out flowers, whilst Lesser's tend to be rather intensely tinged pink or lilac-pink, but flower colour alone is not a reliable distinction. **HABITAT** See Lesser Sea-spurrey. **DISTRIBUTION** Widespread and common in Norfolk, although largely absent from the cliff-bound coasts of the NE of the county and the sandy beaches of the E coast. Occurs around all British coasts.

Key features
- Flowers usually 10-12 mm across (rarely 7-13 mm)
- Sepals 4-6 mm long (occasionally 3.5 mm)
- 10 stamens, rarely fewer
- Seed capsule usually 7-9 mm long, equalling or longer than its stalk
- Most or all seeds have a very broad, flat 'wing' (like the rings of Saturn)

Key facts
- Perennial
- Stems to 40 cm long, more or less sprawling.
- Stems hairless or with sticky hairs around flowers
- Leaves fleshy, cylindrical, pointed
- Flowers 5-petalled, with 3 styles and 10 stamens
- Flowers Jun-Sep

LESSER SEA-SPURREY *Spergularia marina*

Generally the commoner of the two sea-spurreys, and sometimes found inland along salted roads.

IDENTIFICATION Petals shorter than sepals. **HABITAT** Both Greater and Lesser Sea-spurrey are essentially saltmarsh plants, with Greater often commoner in the wetter lower marsh and Lesser more abundant on the higher, drier marsh and alongside paths and other compacted areas around the upper margins. Both species also grow in other saline coastal places, including the damp flats just inland of the shingle bank between Cley and Kelling Hard. Intriguingly, since the late 1970s Lesser Sea-spurrey has spread extensively inland, colonising the margins of main roads that are salted in winter (although to nothing like the extent of Danish Scurvygrass, see p. 29). Greater has also been recorded inland, but only rarely. **DISTRIBUTION** As Greater Sea-spurrey.

Key features
- Flowers usually 5-8 mm in diameter (rarely 4 mm)
- Sepals 2.5-4 mm long.
- Usually 2-7 stamens (rarely 0, or up to 10)
- Seed capsule usually 3-6 mm long, shorter than its stalk
- A variable proportion of seeds (sometimes none) have a 'wing'

Key facts
- Annual, sometimes perennial
- Stems to 35 cm, but more or less sprawling
- Stem hairless at base, usually sticky-hairy towards tip
- Leaves fleshy, cylindrical, pointed
- Flowers 5-petalled, with 3 styles and 2-7 stamens
- Flowers Apr-Sep

SEA CAMPION *Silene uniflora*

One of the signature plants of the shingle bank, growing on the flatter, more stable areas, where its low-growing habit, grey-green foliage and masses of white flowers mark it out.

IDENTIFICATION Resembles Bladder Campion *S. vulgaris*, a common plant of rough grassland and hedge-banks, but mat-forming with fleshy, waxy leaves and larger flowers that are held more erect. **HABITAT** Stabilised shingle or sandy-shingle. **DISTRIBUTION** Common on the north coast, extending from Snettisham to Weybourne, but only found at a few sites further east. Away from Norfolk found around most British coasts (although scarce in NE England), and also occurs rather rarely in mountain habitats.

Key features
- Stems to 30 cm, but usually low-growing
- Flowers 20-25 mm across, white
- Only 1-4 flowers per stem (often just one)
- Flowers held erect
- Teeth at tip of fruit-capsule spreading or down-turned
- Whole plant hairless or only sparsely hairy

Key facts
- Perennial, with both flowering and non-flowering shoots
- Flowers Mar-Oct

SAND CATCHFLY *Silene conica*

A striking plant, with little shocking-pink flowers, but rare in Britain. It is something of a Norfolk speciality, with the most accessible colonies occurring along the N coast.

IDENTIFICATION The vivid flowers, inflated bladders and sticky-hairy leaves and stem are distinctive. **HABITAT** Light sandy soils, usually where disturbed by Rabbits or otherwise kept open; on the coast found in clifftop grassland and alongside paths. **DISTRIBUTION** Its Norfolk (and British) stronghold is in Breckland, but also found very locally on the coast around Sheringham and Old Hunstanton. Nationally scarce, the species is classified as 'Vulnerable' due to its continuing decline.

Key features
- Stems up to 35 cm long, but often sprawling
- Flowers 4-5 mm across, with 5 notched petals, 10 stamens and 3 styles
- Usually only a few flowers open at any one time
- Sepals fused into a calyx-tube that is greyish with 30 or so green ribs; this inflates as the seeds develop to form a 'bladder'
- Leaves grey-green, narrow and pointed, sticky-hairy

Key facts
- Annual, germinating in the spring
- Good seed production occurs only in hot summers
- Flowers May-early Jul

COMMON SEA-LAVENDER *Limonium vulgare*

In mid summer the Norfolk saltmarshes take on a spectacular lavender hue as masses of sea-lavenders come into flower. On a warm summer's day there is nothing to beat it and, even for those with little interest in wildlife, it is a sight well worth searching out.

Key features
- Stems up to 40 cm tall, branching above the centre
- Leaves long-stalked, up to 20 cm long, with branched (pinnate) veins
- Clusters of 1-5 flowers form spikelets, which in turn are grouped into spikes at the end of the branches
- Flower spikes mostly 1-2 cm long, with more than 4 spikelets per cm (and the lowest 2 spikelets 1.5-3 mm apart)
- Flowers 8 mm across, with 5 petals
- Anthers yellow

Key facts
- Perennial, with a tough, woody rootstock
- Pollinated by bees, flies and butterflies
- Sea-lavenders are not related to lavenders, rather they are in the Thrift family, Plumbaginaceae
- Flowers late Jun-early Oct

IDENTIFICATION The slightly fleshy, waxy, strap-shaped leaves form a loose and rather upright rosette at the base of the plant, from which grow sprays of purplish-blue flowers. The papery, pale lilac sepals form a calyx tube which persists long after the petals have fallen. **HABITAT** Muddy saltmarshes, rarely on the stonework of sea walls. **DISTRIBUTION** The Wash, the N coast east to Weybourne, and Breydon Water, also recorded on the NE coast around Walcott and Paston. Occurs north to SW Scotland, but absent from Ireland.

LAX-FLOWERED SEA-LAVENDER *Limonium humile*

The rarest of Norfolk's sea-lavenders and the hardest to identify with certainty.

IDENTIFICATION Rather similar to some variants of Common Sea-lavender but the stems branch below the centre and the flower spikes are longer, with the individual spikelets spaced further apart; anthers reddish-brown. Hybrids and intermediates with Common Sea-lavender also occur (e.g. on Blakeney Point), and this species can only be identified with absolute certainty by a microscopic examination of the pollen. **HABITAT** Muddy saltmarshes. **DISTRIBUTION** Small, scattered populations have been reported from Scolt Head, Wells, Stiffkey and Blakeney Harbour. Norfolk populations are outliers, and the species is otherwise found around the Essex marshes, the Solent, the W coast and Ireland.

Common Sea-lavender: Flower spikes mostly 1-2 cm long, with more than 4 spikelets per cm; anthers yellow

Lax-flowered Sea-lavender: Longest flower spikes 2-5 cm long, with 3 or fewer spikelets per cm; anthers reddish-brown

MATTED SEA-LAVENDER *Limonium bellidifolium*

A real Norfolk speciality, this delicate, low-growing sea-lavender is now found nowhere else in Britain (it formerly occurred in Lincolnshire, but has not been seen there since 1967). It can be locally abundant, with the low-growing plants smothered in pale pink flowers in mid summer.

IDENTIFICATION Multi-branched but leafless when flowering, resembling a giant lichen. **HABITAT** The drier, upper parts of the saltmarsh, on open flats of compacted sand and gravel that are relatively infrequently washed by the tide; often grows together with Sea-heath (p. 28). **DISTRIBUTION** Confined to the N coast between Holme and Blakeney Point, and also recorded on the Wash around Snettisham. Despite its very limited distribution in Britain, not considered threatened.

Key features
- Stems grow to 30 cm, but very bushy, the stems branching from the base
- Flowers only on upper branches
- Flowers 5 mm across
- White, papery bracts conspicuous long after the flowers have withered
- Leaves oblong, 1.5-4 cm long, but withered and brown by flowering time

Key facts
- Perennial
- Insect-pollinated
- Flowers Jul-early Aug

ROCK SEA-LAVENDER *Limonium binervosum*

'Rock Sea-Lavender' is a complex of nine closely related (and very similar) species and 17 subspecies. The Norfolk plants are correctly named as *Limonium binervosum* subspecies *anglicum*, and this subspecies is endemic to Norfolk (it formerly also occurred in Lincolnshire, but is now extinct there).

IDENTIFICATION The flowering stems branch below the centre and arise from a compact rosette

of short leaves, which have short, winged stalks and unbranched veins. **HABITAT** Shingle banks and a narrow zone where the saltmarsh grades into sand dunes.

Key features
- 8-30 cm tall
- Leaves short, less than 10 cm long

Key facts
- Perennial, retaining its leaves through the winter
- Insect-pollinated
- Most members of the complex are found on the S and W coasts
- Flowers Jul-Sep

DISTRIBUTION Locally common on the Wash from Wolferton northwards and the N coast as far east as Salthouse. Rock Sea-lavenders in general are widespread around the coasts of S Britain and Ireland.

CURLED DOCK *Rumex crispus*

Docks are all-too-familiar garden weeds but one also makes its home along the coast. This is subspecies *littoreus* of Curled Dock, which flowers early in the season, leaving its russet-brown, seed-covered dead stems to stand guard over the shingle for the rest of the summer.

IDENTIFICATION Distinguished from other docks by the strap-shaped, wavy-edged leaves and the fruits, which are enclosed by three tepals, each 4-5 mm long, triangular to egg-shaped and untoothed. On inland plants often just one of these tepals carries a large raised wart, but in subspecies *littoreus* all three have a wart, and this subspecies also has denser sprays of fruits. **HABITAT** Very varied, from arable fields to waste ground, but subspecies *littoreus* is confined to shingle by the sea. **DISTRIBUTION** Subspecies *littoreus* is abundant on Blakeney Point and also recorded from Holme and Wells. Elsewhere it occurs scattered around all coasts, being scarcest in SE England. The typical form is found as a weed throughout the British Isles, including Norfolk.

Key features
- Stems to 1 m
- The little flowers have 6 green, sepal-like tepals, the outer 3 tiny, the inner 3 broader and enlarging in fruit to enclose the nut

Key facts
- Perennial
- Flowers May-Oct; plants on the shingle bank are usually all early

THRIFT *Armeria maritima*

One of the most delightful seaside plants, usually associated with wild, windswept cliff tops in the west of Britain but equally at home on Norfolk's saltmarshes.

IDENTIFICATION The leaves form untidy, cushion-like rosettes, from which grow the unique pompom-like flower heads, the flowers varying from white to pink. **HABITAT** The drier parts of well-vegetated saltmarshes and adjacent open areas of compacted sand and shingle; also cliffs and clifftop grassland. **DISTRIBUTION** The Wash, the N coast east to Sheringham, and the E coast between Bacton and Happisburgh. Occasionally found inland, but these probably originate from escaped garden cultivars. Widespread around all British coasts, and also occurs inland very locally in the uplands and on lead mining spoil and river shingle.

Key features
- Flower stems unbranched, 5-30 cm tall
- Flower-heads pompom-like, 15-25 mm wide, the individual flowers just 8 mm across
- Leaves fleshy, very narrow (less than 2 mm wide), 2-10 cm long

Key facts
- Perennial, growing from a tough woody rootstock and retaining its leaves through the winter
- Insect pollinated
- Also known as Sea Pink.
- Flowers late Apr-Jul, with smaller numbers to Oct

SEA-HEATH *Frankenia laevis*

This mat-forming plant is not a heath at all, rather it is the only British member of the Frankeniaceae, a family of salt-tolerant plants that is found across six continents, but has its headquarters in the Mediterranean. Sea-heath is the most northerly member of the family, and Norfolk and Lincolnshire hold the most northerly colonies in the world.

IDENTIFICATION The prostrate stems and tiny, strap-shaped leaves recall a low-growing heather, but the delicate, papery, five-petalled pink flowers are distinctive. **HABITAT** Rather bare, open areas of compacted sand and fine gravel in the zone between the saltmarsh and the sand dunes. **DISTRIBUTION** Confined to the N coast between Titchwell and Blakeney Point, rather sparsely distributed, but can be locally common. Formerly found further west, to Heacham on the Wash. Classified as 'Near-threatened' in Britain, the species occurs from Lincolnshire to the Isle of Wight, with other records in SW Britain attributed to garden escapes (it is sometimes grown in rock gardens).

Key features
- Leaves 3-7 mm long with inrolled margins
- Stems fine but tough and wiry, up to 35 cm long
- Flowers 5-6 mm across, with 5 petals, 6 stamens (arranged in 2 whorls) and a 3-lobed stigma.
- Compare with sea-spurreys (p. 18-19)

The combination of 5 crinkled pink petals and 6 stamens is unique.

Key facts
- Perennial
- Leaves remain green through the winter
- Flowers pollinated by hoverflies
- Seed production may be poor, especially in small, isolated populations, but new plants may be produced by 'layering'
- Flowers Jun-Sep

ENGLISH SCURVY-GRASS *Cochlearia anglica*

Scurvy-grasses are so-called because of the high vitamin C content of their leaves, and were once widely used in the prevention of scurvy on long sea voyages.

IDENTIFICATION The four-petalled white flowers, up to 16 mm across, and glossy, somewhat fleshy leaves render scurvy-grasses distinctive. There are three species in Norfolk, hard to separate with certainty, but English Scurvy-grass is by far the commonest in coastal habitats and has the lower leaves tapering gradually into the stalk and flattened seed-pods. **HABITAT** Saltmarshes and areas of firm mud near the high-water mark on estuaries and tidal rivers **DISTRIBUTION** The Wash eastwards to Cley, Breydon Water, and the lower reaches of associated rivers. Widespread on British coasts, although absent from most of Scotland.

Key features
- Stems to 40 cm, but often rather straggly
- Lower leaves stalked, forming a rosette, upper leaves sometimes stalkless, clasping the stem

Key facts
- Biennial to perennial
- Leaves edible, but un-pleasantly bitter
- Flowers Apr-Jul

DANISH SCURVY-GRASS *Cochlearia danica*

Scarce on the coast of Norfolk, this saltmarsh species is nevertheless easy to see as it has colonised the verges of roads that are regularly salted in winter. Mar-May look for a narrow band of low-growing white flowers along the edge of the carriageway. Examined closely, the flowers are small (only 4-5 mm across) and often tinged lilac.

SEA ROCKET   *Cakile maritima*

One of the signature plants of the strandline on sandy beaches, where the debris left by winter storms has decayed and added nutrients to the sand.

IDENTIFICATION The pale lilac, four-petalled flowers and shiny, fleshy, blue-green leaves (usually deeply-cut) are unique. **HABITAT** The strandline on sandy beaches, just above the line of debris left by the highest tides, less often on shingle beaches, and also the earliest stages in the development of sand dunes **DISTRIBUTION** Occurs on all British coasts and widespread in Norfolk, with the exception of the inner Wash and the coast between Cley and Sheringham.

Key features
- Stems to 50 cm, usually sprawling at base, but bending upwards towards flowers
- Flowers 6-12 mm across
- Seed capsule 10-25 mm long, formed into 2 unequal segments

Key facts
- Annual, germinating in the spring
- Flowers pollinated by bees and flies
- Seeds dispersed on the tide
- Although related to cultivated Rocket, barely edible due to its very bitter taste
- Flowers Jun-Sep

SEA-KALE *Crambe maritima*

Described as 'abundant' on the coast of North Norfolk at the end of the 18th century, the blanched young shoots were then promoted as a delicacy and presumably as a result Sea Kale declined massively. By 1866 it was described as 'rare' and sadly this handsome plant remains very localised in the county.

IDENTIFICATION The large clumps of fleshy, grey-green, cabbage-like leaves and sprays of handsome white flowers are distinctive. **HABITAT** Shingle banks. **DISTRIBUTION** The Wash coast between Snettisham and Heacham. Seed was sown on Blakeney Point in 1912, but the lone plant that resulted was destroyed in the 1953 storm-surge. Sea Kale then reappeared on the Point between the Hood and the Watch House around 1968 and there are still a few plants in this area. Away from Norfolk it is more-or-less confined to the region between Suffolk and Scilly and to Irish Sea coasts, and is scarce.

Key features
- 40-75 cm tall and up to 100 cm across
- Flowers 10-20 mm across
- Foliage varies from green to purple, but is always hairless and waxen

Young shoots can be cooked like Asparagus, but the population is small and no part of the plant should be gathered.

Key facts
- Long-lived perennial
- Seeds pea-shaped and buoyant, dispersed by the tide; new plants can also grow from root fragments
- Flowers May-Jun

SEA-MILKWORT *Glaux maritima*

A member of the primrose family (Primulaceae), this mat-forming plants repays close examination to appreciate its exquisite flowers.

IDENTIFICATION The tiny flowers lack petals, the colour coming from the pale pink sepals, distinguishing it from Sea-heath (p. 28), Sea Sandwort (p. 17) and the sea-spurreys (pp. 18-19). **HABITAT** Damp, saline and often rather bare ground on the saltmarsh fringe, in dune slacks and behind the shingle bank, penetrating inland along the banks of tidal rivers. **DISTRIBUTION** Common on the Wash, the N coast east to Weybourne, and around Breydon Water, with a few scattered sites in NE Norfolk. Occurs on all British coasts.

Key features
- Sprawling, shoots up to 30 cm long
- Leaves fleshy, strap-shaped but stalkless, 4-12 mm long
- Flowers solitary, 3-5 mm across, in leaf axils
- 5 sepals and 5 stamens; petals absent

Key facts
- Perennial
- Either self-pollinated or pollinated by small flies
- Flowers May-Sep

STONECROPS *Sedum sp.*

Stonecrops are low-growing perennials, and are true succulents, their fleshy leaves being adaptations for survival in parched, arid habitats. Although none is confined to the coast, two species are conspicuous there, forming mats of brilliant yellow or white star-like flowers.

BITING STONECROP
Sedum acre

IDENTIFICATION The yellow flowers, held on short but erect flower spikes, and acrid, peppery-tasting leaves are unique amongst stonecrops. Leaves egg-shaped, bright green, 3-5 mm long; flowers 10-14 mm across. Flowers May-Jul. **HABITAT** Rather bare, dry places: shingle, dunes, short turf, and walls. **DISTRIBUTION** Quite common throughout Norfolk and similarly through the rest of Britain.

ENGLISH STONECROP
Sedum anglicum

IDENTIFICATION Flowers white, with the flower spike typically having two branches, each with 3-6 flowers. Leaves egg-shaped, grey-green, usually tinged red; flowers 4-8 mm across Do not confuse with White Stonecrop *S. album*, a widespread

introduction, which has longer leaves and multi-branched flower spikes. Flowers Jun-Sep. **HABITAT** Clifftop grassland and dunes. **DISTRIBUTION** Scarce and declining in Norfolk, with most records between Blakeney Point and Sheringham. Elsewhere, occurs mostly in W Britain.

COMMON BIRD'S-FOOT TREFOIL *Lotus corniculatus*

Widespread in every sort of rough, dry grassland, this member of the pea family is often very conspicuous on the coast. The leaves, despite having 5 leaflets, are 'three-foiled' (the basal pair are well-separated at the base of the leaf stalk), while the seed pods are indeed remarkably like a bird's foot.

IDENTIFICATION
A perennial, flowering May-Sep. The prostrate stems may reach 50 cm. Flowers yellow (often reddish in bud), with 2-8 per flower-head, 5-lobed leaves and seed pods are distinctive. Greater Bird's-foot Trefoil *L. pedunculatus*, with 5-12 flowers per head, favours damper habitats and is seldom found on the coast. **HABITAT** Grassland, also shingle banks and sand dunes. **DISTRIBUTION** Occurs throughout Norfolk and the British Isles.

KIDNEY VETCH *Anthyllis vulneraria*

Another member of the pea family, named after its large kidney-shaped flower heads, this is one of the most conspicuous plants along the cliffs of NE Norfolk.

IDENTIFICATION A perennial, flowering May-Sep, with sprawling, stems reaching 60 cm. Flower heads paired, 2-4 cm wide, with numerous flowers. These are usually yellow, but can be orange or red; each has an inflated calyx (formed by the fused sepals) that is covered with woolly-white hairs. **HABITAT** Rough grassland, usually on sandy, lime-rich soils, often on sea cliffs. **DISTRIBUTION** In Norfolk more-or-less confined to Breckland and the NE coast between Sheringham and Bacton, with a few sites along the Wash coast; sometimes sown along main roads. Occurs widely across Britain.

SEA PEA *Lathyrus japonicus*

One of the most glamorous of Norfolk's coastal flowers, forming voluptuous mats of grey-green foliage and with large, attractive flowers. Ironically, however, it is not a native to the county, but was introduced by well-meaning naturalists.

IDENTIFICATION Very distinctive, recalling a prostrate Sweet Pea. Note that Norfolk Everlasting Pea *L. heterophyllus*, a garden escape with pinkish-purple flowers, is found in the dunes at Gun Hill. **HABITAT** Shingle beaches. **DISTRIBUTION** Confined to Blakeney Point, where introduced. Seed from Chesil Beach in Dorset was sown at Blakeney Point in 1912, but the resultant plants were thought to have been destroyed by the 1953 storm-surge. 100 seeds collected from Suffolk were then sown by Ted Ellis just west of Cley Coastguards in 1954 and several plant still thrive between Cley and the Watch House. Away from Norfolk, largely restricted to the coast from Suffolk to Dorset, and scarce.

Key features
- Shoots sprawling, up to 1 m long
- Leaves fleshy, blue-green, divided into 2-5 pairs of leaflets
- Flowers initially purple, fading to blue

Key facts
- Long-lived perennial
- Flowers pollinated by bumble-bees
- Seed pods 3-5 cm, recalling a garden pea, and reportedly eaten in Suffolk in times of famine
- Flowers May-Sep

HARE'S-FOOT CLOVER *Trifolium arvense*

A distinctive, widespread and fairly common species in Norfolk, in open grasslands on sandy soils, including road verges, and often conspicuous by the sea. The egg-shaped flower-heads soon elongate into a cylinder that can be up to 25 mm long. Flowers Jun-Sep.

BIRD'S-FOOT CLOVER
Trifolium ornithopodioides

Distinctive, but scarce and easily overlooked, this tiny clover can been found at a few sites on the Norfolk coast. Prefers bare ground produced by trampling and very short turf, including municipal lawns in Sheringham. Flowers in groups of 1-4, white or pale pink and tiny, just 6-8 mm long; leaves hairless. Flowers May-Jul.

SUBTERRANEAN CLOVER
Trifolium subterraneum

The wonderful name is a reference to the seed pods, which are turned down and pushed into the ground as they mature. Found on short turf and bare ground on sandy soils, it is scarce in Norfolk but most records come from the coast between Cley and Sheringham. Similar to Bird's-foot Clover, but flowers larger (8-12 mm long), in groups of 2-5, and accompanied by sterile petal-less flowers; leaves hairy. Flowers May-Jun.

CLUSTERED CLOVER
Trifolium glomeratum

Scarce, with just a few, scattered sites in Norfolk, on bare, sandy places near the sea. One of several similar uncommon clovers, but hairless, with stalkless flower-heads, and with each of the tiny (4-5 mm), purplish-pink flowers projecting from the sepals, whose tips spread star-wise. Flowers Jun-Aug.

SEA-BUCKTHORN *Hippophae rhamnoides*

A spiny shrub up to 3 m high, spreading via suckers and often forming impenetrable thickets. The narrow, strap-shaped leaves are distinctly silvery and the green flowers, which are wind-pollinated and appear before the leaves in the winter or early spring, are tiny, with no petals and just 2 sepals. In the autumn, however, the female bushes may be decked with masses of bright orange berries. Native to the E coast of England, including Norfolk, where it is found on dunes and clifftops, it is widely planted elsewhere, but can be very invasive.

DUKE OF ARGYLL'S TEA-PLANT
Lycium barbarum

Introduced from China in the 17th century, this attractive deciduous shrub has become naturalised in hedges and on walls, often close to the sea. Reaching up to 2.5 m, the slender stems may be spiny and, together with the strap-shaped leaves, is distinctly grey-green. Purplish star-shaped flowers, 10-15 mm across, appear Jun-Sep, followed by oval red berries. The species has recently gained prominence as the source of 'goji berries', long known in Chinese herbal medicine and now promoted as a 'superfood' with amazing antioxidant properties.

TAMARISK *Tamarisk gallica*

An evergreen to deciduous shrub that can grow to 3 m tall, with delicate, feathery foliage; the leaves are reduced to tiny scales that overlap one-another on the twigs. From Jul-Sep sprays of tiny pink flowers appear, each with 5 sepals, petals and stamens and 3 styles. This wind-tolerant shrub, originally from the W Mediterranean, is widely planted by the sea in S England. In Norfolk, where the winters were (formerly) rather cold for the species, there are a few scattered stands, such as on Blakeney Point and by Salthouse duck pond.

ROSE-BAY WILLOWHERB *Chamerion angustifolium*

In the early 19th century this was a rare plant of upland Britain and indeed, in the 1866 *Flora of Norfolk* it was described as 'rare'. Since then, however, it has spread across the whole country. Each plant produces up to 80,000 seeds and its spread was probably aided by the construction of railways and roads, along which the seeds could waft. Rosebay is now abundant, but despite its status as an 'aggressive weed', is a very attractive feature of summer on the Norfolk coast.

IDENTIFICATION Tall, stately spikes of large rose-purple flowers combine with long, pencil-shaped seed-pods which split longitudinally to reveal a mass of white down. **HABITAT** Favours disturbed ground and waste places, often appearing in large numbers after a fire. On the coast conspicuous in many places, but especially in dunes and rough grassland. **DISTRIBUTION** Common throughout Norfolk and similarly ubiquitous throughout in Britain.

Key features
- Grows up to 150 cm tall
- Flowers 20-30 mm across
- 4 petals, unequal in size, and 4 coloured sepals
- Leaves pointed, long and strap-shaped

Key facts
- Perennial
- Pollinated by bees and moths
- Known as 'bombweed' following the Blitz of 1940, as it grew in vast numbers amongst the bombed-out ruins
- Flowers Jun-Sep

SEA SPURGE *Euphorbia paralias*

Spurges are hairless, indeed almost waxen, with simple leaves arranged alternately up the stem and complex green flowers. When broken, the stem exudes a milky sap (but beware, this can be a skin-irritant). Spurges belong to the Euphorbiaceae, a large family with over 5,000 species worldwide, mostly in the tropics (including the Rubber tree), but also including many shrubs adapted to desert conditions.

IDENTIFICATION Multi-stemmed, with blunt, grey-green, fleshy leaves; the main confusion species, Portland Spurge *E. portlandica*, does not occur in Norfolk. **HABITAT** Young dunes and the strandline on sandy beaches. **DISTRIBUTION** Until recently confined to the coast between Old Hunstanton and Wells, with an outpost near Great Yarmouth, but now spreading and extends south on the Wash to Snettisham and also recorded from Bacton in E Norfolk. The county marks its northern limit on the E Coast, but it extends to the Solway in the west and is widespread on the E Coast of Ireland.

Key features
- 20-60 cm tall
- Seeds smooth (pitted in Portland Spurge; seed *capsule* wrinkled in both)

Key facts
- Perennial
- Flowers Jun-Oct

COMMON STORK'S-BILL *Erodium cicutarium*

Stork's-bills are so-called because of the resemblance of their seed pods to a stork's bill. They are distinguished from crane's-bills (the true *Geraniums*) which have similarly beak-like pods, by their pinnately-lobed leaves; in *Geranium* the leaves are palmately-lobed, with the main veins all radiating from the tip of the stalk. Incidentally, the names 'stork's-bill' and 'crane's-bill' imply a familiarity with birds that have been rare in Britain for centuries.

IDENTIFICATION Leaves finely dissected, cut almost to midrib. Two other stork's-bills have been recorded rarely in Norfolk, Musk Stork's-bill *E. moschatum* and formerly Sea Stork's-bill *E. maritimum*, but neither have leaves as finely cut. **HABITAT** Short turf and bare ground on well-drained, often sandy soils, including sand dunes. **DISTRIBUTION** Widespread throughout Norfolk and similarly through Britain, but largely coastal in Ireland.

Key features
- Usually low-growing or prostrate, but stems may straggle to 60 cm
- Whole plant rather sticky-hairy, especially on the coast
- Flowers pinkish-purple to white, 10-18 mm, across, in groups of 3-7
- 'Beak' 15-40 mm long

Key facts
- Annual
- Germinates in autumn
- Flowers Apr-Sep

SEA-HOLLY *Eryngium maritimum*

The stunning plant is an atypical member of the carrot family (the umbellifers, Apiaceae), and is very different from most of its relatives, which include roadside weeds such as Cow Parsley and Alexanders. From the 15th century until the end of the 19th century its roots were dug up by 'eryngo diggers' to be candied and sold as a sweetmeat. This trade surely led to a decline in its range and abundance from which it may still be recovering, as it has recently spread in Norfolk.

IDENTIFICATION Whole plant spiny; the blue-green holly-like leaves have whitish veins and margins and are immediately distinctive. Flowers powder-blue, forming dense, egg-shaped heads which recall a teasel rather than an umbellifer. **HABITAT** Sand dunes, less often shingle. **DISTRIBUTION** Snettisham to Wells, and has recently spread east to Blakeney Point; also scattered on the E coast from Mundesley south to Yarmouth. Found on most British coasts, although now extinct in much of NE England and Scotland.

Key features
- 30-60 cm tall, well-branched and bushy
- Fruits egg-shaped, with hooked bristles

Key facts
- Perennial
- Roots may extend 2 m into the ground
- Flowers Jun-Sep

ALEXANDERS *Smyrnium olusatrum*

Introduced to Britain in Roman times as a pot herb, for many years Alexanders was confined to the immediate vicinity of the coast, perhaps due to a liking for mild winter temperatures. Since the 1990s, however, it has undergone something of an explosion, spreading well inland in Norfolk and reaching near plague-proportions on roadside verges and sea banks near the coast.

IDENTIFICATION A typical umbellifer in size and structure, the combination of dull yellowish flowers and glossy dark green leaves, divided into broad, 3-lobed leaflets, is unique. By early summer the roads are lined with dead skeletons carrying the large, ridged black seeds. **HABITAT** Road verges, sea walls and rough grassland. **DISTRIBUTION** Common in N and E Norfolk, numbers diminishing westwards. Scattered throughout Britain, but the bulk of the population occurs from Norfolk and N Wales southwards.

Key features
- Grows to 150 cm
- Tiny petals dull cream; it is the large yellow-green ovary that gives the flower its colour
- Hairless
- Leaves appear in late autumn and overwinter

Key facts
- Biennial
- A native of S Europe and the Mediterranean region
- Celery-scented, it was widely cultivated until the 18th century
- Almost the whole plant is edible, especially the thicker stems, blanched and cooked like celery
- Flowers Mar-May

COMMON CENTAURY   *Centaurium erythraea*

A member of the gentian family (Gentianaceae), the pink star-like flowers only open fully in sunshine, when they are a conspicuous feature of many dunes and other areas of dry grassland.

IDENTIFICATION The rigidly upright habit (although plants are often very short), strap-shaped leaves and dense heads of bright pink 5-petalled flowers are distinctive. Lesser Centaury *C. pulchellum*, a scarce plant in Norfolk, differs in having short stalks to the flowers; plants of both species may be tiny, so size alone does not help. **HABITAT** Short grassland and bare ground on light, often sandy, soils; often common in dune grassland.**DISTRIBUTION** Scattered in suitable habitat throughout Norfolk and the rest of Britain away from the uplands and the far north.

Key features
- 2-50 cm tall
- Leaves in a basal rosette, with 1-2 higher on the stem
- Flowers 9-15 mm across, unstalked or very short-stalked

Key facts
- Biennial, rarely annual
- Pollinated by insects or self-pollinated
- Flowers Jun-Oct

SEA BINDWEED *Calystegia soldanella*

Bindweeds are the bane of every gardener but this is a well-behaved species, confining itself to the seaside. Many Norfolk populations seem rather reluctant to produce flowers.

IDENTIFICATION The flowers are typical of a bindweed in shape and are pink with 5 white stripes and a yellowish centre. They are similar to those of Field Bindweed *Convolvulus arvensis*, which is locally abundant near the coast, but the leaves of Sea Bindweed are kidney-shaped and distinctly fleshy and the base of the flower (the calyx) is enclosed by pouch-like bracteoles. **HABITAT** The strandline on sandy and shingle beaches, also dunes, both on bare ground and amongst a grassy sward. **DISTRIBUTION** Widespread in Norfolk, although absent from the Wash coast south of Snettisham and largely absent between Salthouse and Happisburgh. Occurs north to the Hebrides and SE Scotland.

Key features
- Stems prostrate, growing up to 1 m long
- Flowers 30-55 mm across

Key facts
- Perennial
- Pollinated by bumble-bees or self-pollinated
- Flowers Jun-Aug

Field Bindweed (right) does not have fleshy, kidney-shaped leaves and the base of the flower is not enclosed by pouch-like bracteoles.

VIPER'S-BUGLOSS *Echium vulgare*

Forming sheets of brightest blue when en masse, its Norfolk stronghold is in Breckland but Viper's-bugloss is also locally conspicuous on the coast. The strange name reflects its rough, bristly feel ('bugloss' derives from the Greek for ox-tongued) and the supposed resemblance of various parts of the plant to a snake; indeed, the fruits, said to resemble an Adder's head, were used as a cure for snake bite (note, however, that the plant is is actually poisonous). **IDENTIFICATION** The whole plant is rather roughly hairy or bristly – the stem is dotted with red-based bristles. The erect, statuesque form, up to 1 m tall, clusters of purplish-pink buds and the bright blue, trumpet-shaped flowers, 10-19 mm long, with projecting purplish stamens, are a distinctive combination. Biennial, flowering Jun-Sep. **HABITAT** Open grassland and bare, disturbed ground on dry, often sandy soils, including clifftop grassland, dunes and shingle beaches. **DISTRIBUTION** Widespread in Britain north to S Scotland, but in Ireland largely confined to the E coast.

HOUND'S-TONGUE
Cynoglossum officinale

The strap-shaped, greyish leaves reminded herbalists of a dog's tongue, hence the name, and hence also its past use as a treatment for dig bites! **IDENTIFICATION** Greyish-green and softly downy to the touch, the plant is said to smell of roasted peanuts. Grows to 30-60 cm, with drooping, rich maroon-red flowers. A biennial, it blooms May-Jun, less often to Aug. **HABITAT** Disturbed ground on light, sandy soils and shingle; unpalatable to grazing animals and often stands proud on short, Rabbit-cropped turf. **DISTRIBUTION** In Norfolk common only in Breckland, on the Wash coast and the N coast east to Blakeney Point. Found north to S Scotland but commonest in SE England.

BUCK'S-HORN PLANTAIN *Plantago coronopus*

So-called because the leaves are usually deeply-cut, with short, pointed side-branches (themselves sometimes deeply cut), resembling the tines on a deer's antlers. This unassuming plant is one of the most successful and adaptable, able to tolerate quite a bit of trampling, and is common in many places.

IDENTIFICATION
Distinguished from other plantains by its deeply-cut leaves (but occasionally only slightly toothed), with a single vein on the underside of each segment. **HABITAT** Favours light, sandy or gravelly soils, on bare ground around tracks and paths, on close-cropped turf, dunes, and shingle, and also the edge of saltmarshes. **DISTRIBUTION** Common around the whole coast, but also occurring inland, especially in Breckland and around Norwich. Similarly essentially coastal over most of Britain although widespread inland in SE England.

Key features
- Leaves form a flat rosette, very variable in size, sometimes tiny
- Flowering stem up to 20 cm high, flower spike up to 4 cm long
- Flowers brown, with yellow stamens
- Whole plant usually downy

Key facts
- Annual or short-lived perennial
- Retains its leaves through the winter
- Wind-pollinated
- Flowers May-Oct

SEA PLANTAIN *Plantago maritima*

Together with Thrift and Sea Campion this hardy species, clearly well-adapted to tough conditions, grows in mountainous habitats in N and W Britain as well as on the coast, where it is a common plant in saltmarshes.

IDENTIFICATION Distinguished from other plantains by the erect, narrowly strap-shaped, thick, fleshy leaves. Easily mistaken for the unrelated Sea Arrowgrass (see p. 54) but has broader leaves and denser flower spikes, with each of the close-packed flowers having, when fresh, its 4 stamens projecting on long filaments. **HABITAT** Saltmarshes, but occasionally found in brackish grassland and around cliffs and sea defences. **DISTRIBUTION** Common on the Wash, along the N coast as far east as Blakeney and around Breydon Water, but much more scattered in the intervening area where the habitat is less suitable. Occurs around all British coasts.

Key features
- Grows to 30 cm tall
- Flowering stem up to 30 cm high, flower spike 2-7 cm long
- Whole plant more or less hairless
- Flowers tiny, brown, with conspicuous yellow stamens

Key facts
- Perennial
- Wind-pollinated
- Flowers Jun-Sep

BROOMRAPES *Orobanche* sp.

Fascinating plants, broomrapes have no chlorophyll and lack green coloration; their leaves being merely brownish scales. Unable to manufacture their own food, they are parasites and attach themselves to the roots of other plants. The erect spikes of tubular flowers attract attention and the persistent dead flower spikes are conspicuous well into the winter. Three species are found in Norfolk.

YARROW BROOMRAPE *O. purpurea*

An annual or short-lived perennial that is parasitic on Yarrow *Achillea millefolium*. Rare in Britain and classified as 'Vulnerable', Norfolk is its stronghold, but even here it is scarce and confined to a few grassland sites on or near the clifftops from Sheringham to Mundesley, as well as a very few road verges. Stems up to 45 cm tall, tinged blue, flowers bluish-violet, stigma white, sometimes tinged blue. Flowers late May-Aug.

KNAPWEED BROOMRAPE *O. elatior*

Parasitic on Greater Knapweed *Centaurea scabiosa* and found at scattered sites on chalky grassland, both inland and on the N coast. Stems yellowish to orange-brown, robust, up to 75 cm tall, flowers honey-coloured with yellow stigmas. Flowers Jun-Jul. Perennial.

COMMON BROOMRAPE *O. minor*

Parasitic on a wide variety of plants and widespread throughout Norfolk in a variety of habitats, from clifftop grassland to set-aside or even shrubberies in supermarket car parks and beside main roads. Very variable in size and coloration, it can appears in large numbers. Stems usually distinctly reddish or purplish, up to 60 cm tall (but often quite short), flowers yellowish, veined with purple, stigma purple or, less often, yellow. Flowers Jun-Sep.

LADY'S BEDSTRAW *Galium verum*

A sprawling, low-growing perennial that is honey-scented when fresh but smells of new-mown hay when dry. It was formerly believed to discourage fleas and incorporated into straw mattresses, especially for the beds of women about to give birth, hence its name.

IDENTIFICATION The tiny 4-petalled flowers, 2-3 mm across, appear Jun-Sep. Unique among the bedstraws in having yellow flowers and being quite smooth – it lacks the tiny hooks on leaves and stem that are so well-developed in Cleavers *G. aparine*, a close relative that is the bane of every gardener. Crosswort *Cruciata laevipes* has similar flowers, but is distinguished by having them arranged into clusters around the base of the leaves. **HABITAT** Short grassland on well-drained, infertile, often sandy soils, including dune grassland; also roadside verges. **DISTRIBUTION** Occurs throughout Norfolk, though most abundantly in Breckland and by the sea, and similarly widespread in Britain.

SHEEP'S-BIT *Jasione montana*

The pompoms of pale blue flowers catch the eye, but this member of the bellflower family is scarce in Norfolk and most likely to be found on the E coast.

IDENTIFICATION Biennial, growing to 50 cm, with a rosette of strap-shaped leaves at the base of the stem as well as shorter stalkless leaves higher up. The rounded flower-heads, 10-35 mm across and formed by many small, close-packed flowers, appear Jun-Sep. Similar to Devil's-bit Scabious *Succisa pratensis* but the tiny flowers have five well-separated petals, rather than four petals fused into a tube for most of their length. **HABITAT** Grassland and heathland, including dunes, on acid soils. **DISTRIBUTION** The E coast from Horsey to Gt Yarmouth, with scattered outliers on the N coast (e.g. Blakeney Point). Elsewhere, mostly found in W Britain and numbers in the SE have declined significantly.

GREAT LETTUCE *Lactuca virosa*

Of the many dandelion relatives to be found on the coast, this is the tallest and most statuesque (although the flowers are small and insignificant), and even when dead in late summer the stems stand guard over many Norfolk dunes. It is closely related to the garden lettuce, but the leaves are thick and waxy with a conspicuous row of prickles along the midrib below, and when broken, the plant exudes a milky sap.

IDENTIFICATION Only likely to be confused with Prickly Lettuce *L. serriola*, but that species has leaves with a whitish midrib and spreading, arrow-shaped basal lobes, smaller flowers, and smaller, dull greenish-grey seeds. **HABITAT** Native to coastal grassland, also an increasing introduction to disturbed ground inland, often spreading with road developments. **DISTRIBUTION** Common along the Wash coast and eastward to Wells, more scattered elsewhere in Norfolk. Nationally, confined to S and E England.

Key features
- Erect, to 2 m tall, stems usually tinged maroon, especially towards base
- Leaf and leaf-midribs usually tinged maroon
- Base of leaves tightly clasping stem, basal lobes rounded
- Flowers 15-17 mm across when fully open.
- Seeds 4-5 mm long, purple-black or very dark maroon, drying to black

Key facts
- Annual or biennial
- Flowers Jun-Sep

SEA ASTER *Aster tripolium*

Closely related to garden asters and similarly flowering in the early autumn, towards Michaelmas (29th September), this is one of the signature plants of the Norfolk coast. It occurs in two forms: var. *tripolium*, with lilac ray-florets, is typical of areas not regularly washed by the tide, while the ray-less var. *discoideus* is found on saltmarshes.

IDENTIFICATION Var. *tripolium* is distinctive, and although various garden Michaelmas daisies are established in the wild, none of them likes saline habitats. Var. *discoideus*, with plain yellow flowers, is less distinct, but nothing similar grows in the same habitat. **HABITAT** Saltmarshes, also brackish ditches and wet ground by the sea; around the Wash and Breydon Water, occurs frequently on ground that was once saline, but has long been drained. **DISTRIBUTION** The Wash, the N coast as far east as Weybourne and around Breydon Water and its associated rivers. Widespread around all British coasts.

Key features
- Erect, 15-100 cm tall
- Whole plant hairless and somewhat fleshy
- Leaves strap-shaped
- Flowers 12-20 mm across (8-10 mm in var. *discoideus*)

Key facts
- Usually perennial
- Pollinated by a wide variety of insects
- Flowers Aug-Oct, but often a few plants start blooming from June onwards

var. *discoideus*

SEA WORMWOOD   *Seriphidium maritimum*

The delicate, feathery, grey foliage of this herb is a characteristic feature of the Norfolk saltmarshes. Rub your fingers through the leaves and you will find that the plant is very strongly aromatic. The volatile oils that produce this aroma have various medicinal properties, but are toxic if taken in any quantity – its close relative, Wormwood *Artemisia absinthium*, an ancient introduction to Britain, is the source of the potent drink absinthe.

IDENTIFICATION The finely cut foliage and strong aroma are distinctive. **HABITAT** The higher, drier parts of the saltmarsh as well as nearby sea-walls and rough ground. **DISTRIBUTION** Mostly found on the N coast between Old Hunstanton and Weybourne and around Breydon Water, with scattered sites on the Wash and E coast. Occurs around most British coasts, but absent in the N and W.

Key features
- Stems more or less erect, 20-50 cm tall, often woody at base
- Flowers tiny, yellow or reddish, 1.5-3.5 mm across
- Leaves finely dissected, downy, pale silvery-grey both above and below

Key facts
- Perennial
- Wind-pollinated
- Flowers Aug-Sep

COMMON RAGWORT
Senecio jacobaea

This common weed can be very conspicuous on the coast, lining roadsides as well as occurring in more natural habitats such as dunes and clifftop grassland. Plants are often infested with the yellow and black striped caterpillars of the Cinnabar moth. **IDENTIFICATION** Grows to 30-150 cm. The flat-topped clusters of yellow, daisy-like flowers, each 15-25 mm across, and sombre green, well-divided leaves are distinctive. A biennial or perennial, it flowers Jun-Nov. **HABITAT** Dunes, road verges, neglected pastures and waste ground. **DISTRIBUTION** Occurs throughout Britain, including Norfolk.

STICKY GROUNDSEL *Senecio viscosus*

One of the most conspicuous plants of Norfolk's shingle banks and beaches. **IDENTIFICATION** Rather like Common Groundsel *S. vulgaris*, the familiar garden weed, but distinctively sticky-hairy all over; the flowers have short yellow ray florets but these quickly turn under. Grows to 60 cm, but shingle plants are usually rather shorter. Annual, flowering Jul-Sep. **HABITAT** Bare and waste ground, especially close to the sea. **DISTRIBUTION** Introduced to Britain, it is widespread nationally and occurs throughout Norfolk, but is especially common on the shingle bank between Blakeney Point and Kelling and on the Wash coast (and these maritime populations could actually be native).

SEA ARROWGRASS *Triglochin maritimum*

Although it resembles a grass or rush, this common saltmarsh plant is not very closely related to these groups (being closer to pondweeds). Examined closely the tiny flowers are often a delicate shade of lilac.

IDENTIFICATION The long, slender leaves and spikes of tiny flowers are useful pointers. Easy to confuse with Sea Plantain (p. 47) but has narrower leaves and looser flower spikes, with each flower well separated, short-stalked and, when fresh, with a finely tufted top-knot **HABITAT** Saltmarshes, less commonly on other damp ground by the sea. **DISTRIBUTION** Common in parts of the Wash, on the N coast east to Weybourne, and around Breydon Water, and also found at a few sites in NE Norfolk. Elsewhere, occurs on all British and Irish coasts.

Key features
- Stems erect, to 60 cm
- Leaves all arising from the base, long and very narrow, flat and fleshy
- Flowers tiny, varying in colour from green to purple, with a relatively large ovary topped by a finely tufted stigma
- Ripe fruits held erect and conspicuous, oval, 4-5 mm long

Key facts
- Perennial
- Wind-pollinated
- Flowers May-Sep

flowers

developing fruits

SEASIDE RUSHES, SEDGES & GRASSES

Rushes, sedges and grasses are often rather difficult to identify, but several species occur by the seaside that are either very distinctive, or are found in such numbers (and often in such distinct zones) that they cannot fail to attract attention.

SEA CLUB-RUSH *Bolboschoenus maritimus*

Common on the N coast from Old Hunstanton to Weybourne, and on the Wash and Breydon Water and their associated rivers. Often conspicuous in coastal ditches and pools.

SEA RUSH *Juncus maritimus* (left)

Confined to saltmarshes and ditches near the sea, mostly on the N coast from Old Hunstanton to Cley and around Breydon Water. A tall, conspicuous rush that usually looks rather tatty and which forms a distinct band of greyish vegetation along the upper margins of the saltmarsh.

SHARP RUSH *Juncus acutus*

Essentially a Mediterranean rush, in Britain it is commonest in the SW and is rare in Norfolk. Where it does occur, on the brackish fringes of dunes at Titchwell, Burnham Deepdale and Brancaster, it forms conspicuous large well-spaced tussocks. The leaves have very sharp tips, but those of Sea Rush are also pointed; fruit size, shape and colour are a better guide.

MARRAM
Ammophila arenaria

Found along almost the entire Norfolk coast and equally widespread around Britain, this perennial grass is well-known as a dune-builder, binding the shifting sands together with its amazingly long, tough, underground rhizomes. As the stem and leaves are covered by blown sand, new shoots are produced further up the stem. Marram forms compact tussocks 50-120 cm tall, the individual leaves are up to 100 cm long, stiff and sharply-pointed, with their edges tightly inrolled in dry weather; when it is damp, the leaves flatten out. The cigar-shaped flower spike is produced Jul-Aug and is 7-22 cm long, densely packed with many narrow spikelets.

LYME-GRASS *Leymus arenarius*

Instantly recognisable by its broad, distinctly blue-grey leaves, which may be up to 25 mm wide. Indeed, this large perennial grass may reach 200 cm tall, with the leaves 60 cm or more long. It occurs along most of the Norfolk coast, although it is

absent from the inner Wash and the N coast between Wells and Weybourne and in many places is rather localised, forming rather limited patches. The species favours sandy soils and often grows at the foot or on the seaward side of dunes. The flower spikes are 15-35 cm long and produced Jun-Aug, with the spikelets 20-32 mm long and paired, the pairs arranged into 2 opposite alternate rows up the stem. Many Norfolk plants, however, produce few or no flowers due to the presence of a smut fungus.

SEA COUCH *Elytrigia atherica*

Common along most of the Norfolk coast by brackish creeks, on the higher and drier saltmarsh margins, dunes, shingle banks and sea walls, this perennial grass also penetrates inland from the Wash and Breydon Water along the major rivers, where its range extends beyond the influence of tidal waters. Grows up to 1.2 m tall, forming both tufts and extensive, dense stands, excluding all other vegetation. Variable in colour, but often rather blue-green. The flower spikes appear Jul-Sep and are 4-20 cm long, with the individual spikelets 10-20 mm long, arranged into two rows on opposite sides of the stem, and usually closely overlapping.

SAND COUCH *Elytrigia juncea*

Rather similar to Sea Couch, this is a pioneer species and the first plant to colonise fresh sand, growing close to the sea, on or just above the strandline on sandy or shingle beaches. It may build low fore-dunes, but also grows on more stabilised dunes together with Marram and Sea Couch. It occurs in small numbers along most of the Norfolk coast, but is absent from the stretch between Cley and East Runton. Growing up to 80 cm tall, it forms loose tufts or mats and is distinctly bluish-grey. The flower spikes appear Jun-Aug and are similar to those of Sea Couch, although the individual spikelets are larger, at 15-28 mm, and spaced more or less their own length apart and thus hardly overlapping. The two species can be hard to separate and do hybridise, but using a hand lens it can be seen that the ribs on the upperside of the leaf are densely hairy in Sand Couch.

Sand Couch

Sea Couch

COMMON CORD-GRASS *Spartina anglica*

A common and conspicuous grass of the saltmarsh, and a plant which has a strange genesis. Around 1870 Small Cord-grass *S. maritima*, a British native, hybridised with Smooth Cord-grass *S. alterniflora* (accidentally introduced from North America), to produce the hybrid Townsend's Cord-grass *S. x townsendii*. Although sterile, Townsend's Cord-grass spread rapidly, but then around 1890, via a process of chromosome doubling, it gave rise to Common Cord-grass *S. anglica*, a new, fully fertile species. Now Townsend's Cord-grass has begun to disappear, perhaps in the face of competition from its fertile offspring, and Common Cord-grass is the only species found in Norfolk.

IDENTIFICATION A robust grass which often forms dense swards and which, when in flower, has its anthers and stigmas conspicuously dangling. **HABITAT** Tidal mudflats and saltmarshes. **DISTRIBUTION** Confined to the Wash and the N coast east to Kelling, with a couple of records from the E coast. Nationally, found on muddy shores north to S Scotland.

Key features
- Grows up to 130 cm tall, although usually rather shorter in Norfolk
- Leaves broad, 6-15 mm wide

Key facts
- Deciduous, perennial
- Wind-pollinated, as are all grasses
- Cord-grasses have been planted in the past to aid the reclamation of mudflats
- Flowers Jul-Nov

Grasses are flowering plants, but as they are wind-pollinated, they do not need to attract insects with conspicuous or scented flowers. They merely dangle their anthers (left) to shed pollen, which is dispersed by the wind and intercepted by the large, feathery stigmas (right).

COMMON REED *Phragmites australis*

Often referred to as 'Norfolk Reed', this iconic plant is conspicuous on much of the coast, thanks to a tolerance of brackish conditions, and often forms extensive, dense reedbeds.

IDENTIFICATION Stout, rigid stems, broad leaves and large soft, feathery purplish-brown flower heads distinctive. The stems and seed heads persist through the winter. Separated from the somewhat similar Reed Canary-grass *Phalaris arundinacea* by having a ligule at the base of the leaves formed by a dense fringe of short hairs rather than a membranous flap. **HABITAT** Grows wherever there is wet ground or standing water, including ditches and marshes by the sea. **DISTRIBUTION** Found throughout Norfolk and similarly widespread throughout Britain.

Key features
- Up to 350 cm tall
- Leaves up to 5 cm wide
- Flower heads 20-60 cm long, each floret surrounded by tufts of silky white hairs

Key facts
- Perennial, growing from tough creeping rhizomes
- Reedbeds are an important habitat for several birds, notably Bittern and Bearded Tit
- Cut in the winter months to provide reed for thatching
- Flowers Aug-Oct

Thatch was the commonest roof covering in Britain until the end of the medieval period and remained so in many rural areas until the mid 19th Century. The materials used for thatching were those readily at hand. Wheat straw was the most widely used, but 'Norfolk' or 'Water' Reed was used in East Anglia and other regions with suitable wetlands, and each region evolved a particular style of thatching. Wheat straw (from old-fashioned, long-stemmed varieties) is still used, but reed is more durable – a roof thatched with reed, and with the steep pitch traditional in East Anglia, should last an average of 50-60 years.

MARSH HELLEBORINE *Epipactis palustris*

One of the most attractive British orchids. When examined closely the flowers, though small, are miniature versions of the glamorous tropical hybrid orchids that are now widely available.

IDENTIFICATION Easily identified by the complex green and white flowers, with a frilly lip and pinkish-purple veining. **HABITAT** Dune slacks and, away from the coast, fens flushed by chalky, lime-rich water. **DISTRIBUTION** On the coast, large colonies can be found at Holme, Wells and Holkham. Occurs at scattered sites in Britain, including Norfolk, north to S Scotland.

Key features
- Usually 20-45 cm tall
- Leaves broadly strap-shaped, pointed, with prominent veins and a distinct keel
- Each spike has up to 25 flowers, all facing more or less the same way

Key facts
- Perennial, growing from a network of rhizomes
- Pollinated by insects
- As in all orchids, the flower is made up of 3 sepals and 3 petals, one of which is specially modified and forms the 'lip'
- Flowers Jul, sometimes from late Jun or into early Aug

EARLY MARSH ORCHID
Dactylorhiza incarnata

A scarce and declining orchid, especially the typical subspecies, which has pale pink flowers, and is found scattered in marshes and wet meadows in Norfolk and throughout Britain. On the coast, however, the distinctive subspecies *coccinea*, with deep red flowers, can occur in large numbers. Endemic to the British Isles, *coccinea* is essentially a plant of dunes slacks on the W coast and the *machair* grasslands of the Western Isles, but there are a couple of large colonies in Norfolk, at Holme and on the wet, slippery, slumped clay cliffs at Overstrand; at the latter site odd plants can even be found dislodged at the base of the cliffs, in danger of being washed away by the tide. Looking like a fat little hyacinth, *coccinea* flowers late Jun-Jul.

SOUTHERN MARSH ORCHID *Dactylorhiza praetermissa*

By far the commonest marsh orchid in Norfolk (and S Britain), this species is often found in large numbers, in wet meadows, marshes and dune slacks (but also sometimes in dry grassland). On the Norfolk coast there are large colonies at Gun Hill, Holkham and Wells. The whole plant is usually rather robust, 20-50 cm tall (or even as much as 70 cm), with a stout stem and numerous unmarked leaves. The flowers are purplish-pink with a broad, rounded lip that has a tooth-like central lobe. Flowers late May-early Jul.

PYRAMIDAL ORCHID *Anacamptis pyramidalis*

The cerise-pink flowers of this orchid catch the eye when growing amidst the sombre grasses of the sand dunes.

IDENTIFICATION Flower spikes densely packed with unmarked, bright pink flowers, conical at first (hence the name) but becoming globular or cylindrical as more flowers open. The colour and shape of the spikes are distinctive, although Red Valerian *Centranthus ruber*, a common garden plant often naturalised on walls, is superficially similar. **HABITAT** Dry, well-drained grassland on calcareous soils, including lime-rich dunes and road verges. **DISTRIBUTION** Quite uncommon in Norfolk, but some good colonies on the N coast between Hunstanton and Wells. Occurs north to S Scotland, but most widespread in SE England.

Key features
- Usually 20-60 cm tall
- Leaves strap-shaped with a pointed tip, decreasing in size up the stem and often withering by Jun
- Flowers have a deeply 3-lobed lip and a very long, thin, down-curved spur
- Some plants have pale pink flowers

Key facts
- Perennial
- Pollinated by moths and butterflies
- Flowers mid Jun-mid Jul

BEE ORCHID
Ophrys apifera

An exotic and exciting orchid, this is one of hundreds of species in the genus *Ophrys* that have evolved flowers to attract male bees and wasps by mimicking the look, feel and even the scent of a female bee or wasp. The unwitting males then pollinate the flowers. Unlike all the other *Ophrys*, however, the Bee Orchid has abandoned sex and is self-pollinated.

IDENTIFICATION
Very distinctive and quite unmistakable. **HABITAT** Sparsely vegetated, poor and usually rather dry soils, including dunes, road verges and, increasingly in N Norfolk, unfertilised garden lawns. **DISTRIBUTION** Scattered throughout Norfolk. On the coast found in grasslands in the NE and in dune slacks from Wells westwards. Widely distributed in Britain north to Cumbria and Co Durham.

Key features
- 10-45 cm tall
- Leaves strap-shaped, becoming narrower and more pointed up the stem
- Leaves appear in autumn and are often scorched by flowering time

Key facts
- Perennial
- Flowers Jun, sometimes from late May or into Jul

INDEX